Essential Co

COMPREHENSIVE, STEP BY STEP COOKING

Oriental
Cooking

BUDGET
BD
D
BOOKS

Food Editor: Neil Hargreaves
Cover Design: Budget Books
Prepress: Graphic Print Group

BUDGET BOOKS Essential Cooking Series: Oriental Cooking
First published in 2008 by Budget Books Pty Ltd
45–55 Fairchild Street
Heatherton, Victoria, 3202, Australia

10 9 8 7 6
13 12 11 10 09

Disclaimer: The nutritional information listed under each recipe does not
include the nutrient content of garnishes or any accompaniments not listed
in specific quantitites in the ingredient list. The nutritional information for
each recipe is an estimate only, and may vary depending on the brand of
ingredients used, and due to natural biological variations in the composition
of natural foods such as meat, fish, fruit and vegetables. The nutritional
information was calculated by using Foodworks dietary analysis software
(Version 3, Xyris Software Pty Ltd, Highgate Hill, Queensland, Australia) based
on the Australian food composition tables and food manufacturers' data.
Where not specified, ingredients are always analysed as average or medium,
not small or large.

ISBN: 978 1 7418 1466 8

Printed and bound in China

Contents

An introduction to Oriental cooking

Eastern food is becoming increasingly popular throughout the Western world. Chinese restaurants are now being joined by Thai and Japanese restaurants that serve a variety of different Asian dishes. Oriental cooking encompasses a vast range of food styles, from the spicy curries of South-East Asia to the natural tastes of Japanese sushi. Each country has its own unique way of cooking and its native ingredients. They do, however, have some things in common. The food is usually simply prepared, healthy and packed full of flavour – and often cooked in a wok.

The wok originated in China and is now the main cooking utensil in most Asian countries. It's also being used in many Western countries because of the unique way in which it cooks food.

In Indonesia, the wok is called a kuali or wajan. The Malay version is also a kuali, and in Vietnam it's called a chao. Today there are a variety of woks available: flat-based woks are best suited to electric hotplates, and electric woks have a built-in element. The general shape is the same in all woks, the wide open area being perfect for quick, even cooking of food.

The wok is one of the most versatile pieces of cooking equipment. It can be used for stir-frying, deep-frying, steaming, braising and boiling. For someone just setting up a kitchen, it's a great investment. The best woks are often inexpensive, and the more a wok is used, the better it is to cook in.

HOW TO STIR-FRY

Before you start stir-frying, you have to keep one thing in mind: speed is the most important thing. Why? Because stir-frying is designed for quick cooking. This not only makes your food taste great, it also preserves the colour and aroma of the ingredients. You always have to stir-fry on the highest heat possible – at the oil's smoking point – to achieve the quickest stir-fry possible. Follow these simple steps to the perfect stir-fry every time:

- Prepare your ingredients ahead of time. That includes washing and chopping up.
- Add a good amount of oil into the wok: 3–5 tablespoons is recommended.
- Turn the heat on to its highest point, and wait until the oil reaches smoking point.
- Add any spices you have first, such as garlic, ginger or chillies.
- Add your ingredients according to density.

You can pretty much use any type of cooking pot or pan, but a wok is preferred for stir-frying. You'll also need some type of spatula – a stainless steel one is best, unless you're

using a non-stick wok or pan. In this case, you should use a wooden or plastic spatula. You can even use chopsticks to stir-fry, if you're good at handling them. You also need a decent stove that can generate lots of heat. Gas stoves are the best, since you have better and quicker control over the heat than you do with electric stoves.

Always stir-fry meat first after your spices. If you plan to fry dense veggies such as broccoli or cauliflower, blanche or parboil them first. Stir-fry to the point where the ingredients are just cooked, and no longer, and serve while hot. Follow these simple stir-fry steps, and you can stir-fry like a pro!

CARING FOR YOUR WOK

Before using a new wok, it's important to season it. First, wash it well with hot water and detergent, to remove any coating. If the coating is a lacquer, fill the wok with cold water and 2 tablespoons of bicarbonate

of soda and boil it for 15 minutes, before removing the coating with a fine scourer. The wok is then ready to be seasoned. To do this, place your wok over the heat, pour in 2 tablespoons of oil and add some chopped spring onions and garlic cloves. Stir-fry these ingredients over a moderate heat for 2–3 minutes, covering the whole wok surface. Throw out the mixture and wash the wok in warm water. Wipe it out with kitchen towels and rub a fine film of oil over the inside.

After seasoning a wok, never use anything abrasive to clean it. After every use, fill the wok with water, then wash it in soapy water. Always dry the wok well and wipe it out with a little oil before storing. Cooking in a wok is good for quick family meals. It's also great for entertaining, because with stir-frying, most of the work is in the preparation and this can all be done in advance before the guests arrive.

ASIAN INGREDIENTS

Bamboo shoots: These are the young edible shoots of certain kinds of bamboo. Available, canned, from Asian food stores and some supermarkets, they are pale yellow in colour and have a crunchy texture.

Black beans: Also known as salted black beans, these are small black soy beans. Their unique flavour is achieved by fermenting them with salt and spices. They have a slightly salty taste and a rich smell, and are usually used as a seasoning. Available, canned, from Asian food stores. If leftover beans are stored in an airtight container in the refrigerator they will keep indefinitely.

Chilli paste (sambal oelek): This is a paste of chillies and salt that can be used as an ingredient or condiment.

Chilli sauce: Chinese chilli sauce is a bright red, hot sauce made from chillies, vinegar, sugar and salt. Sometimes used in cooking, it is most popular as a dipping sauce for foods such as spring rolls and wontons. For those who find this sauce too strong, try diluting it with a little hot water.

Chinese dried mushrooms: These are fairly expensive, but a few will add a unique flavour to any dish. To use dried mushrooms, place mushrooms in a bowl, cover with hot water and set aside to soak for about 20 minutes or until soft. Squeeze out excess liquid, remove tough stems and use as required. For added flavour, the soaking liquid is often added to dishes.

Egg noodles: The flat Oriental noodles are often used in soups, while the round noodles are served with sauces and are best for stir-fries. They are also served as an accompaniment, instead of rice.

Fish sauce: This is the drained liquid from salted fermented anchovies. It is an essential ingredient in Thai and Vietnamese cooking.

Five-spice powder: This pungent, fragrant, spicy and slightly sweet powder is a mixture of star anise, Szechuan peppercorns, fennel, cloves and cinnamon.

Garam masala: An aromatic spice mixture, comprising of up to 20 different spices. Differs from the commercial curry powder in the omission of the pungent, bright spice turmeric.

Glutinous rice: This round-grained rice is used for stuffings and desserts. If it is unavailable, short-grain or pudding rice can be used in its place.

Hoisin sauce: Also known as Chinese barbecue sauce, this is a thick dark brown sauce made from soy beans, vinegar, sugar, spices and other flavourings. It has a sweet spicy flavour and is mainly used in southern Chinese cooking.

Lotus root: In India and China the lotus plant is considered to be sacred. Lotus root, as the name suggests, is the root of the lotus plant and is perforated with holes. It is used extensively as a garnish in Chinese and Japanese cooking. It is available canned or dried. When using dried lotus root, first soak it in hot water with 1/2 teaspoon lemon juice for 20 minutes.

Oyster sauce: Made from a concentrate of oysters cooked in soy sauce and brine, oyster sauce is dark brown in colour and has a rich flavour. It is used both in cooking and as a condiment.

Plum sauce: A popular dipping sauce, plum sauce is made from plums preserved in vinegar, sugar, chillies and spices.

Rice noodles: Also called rice vermicelli or rice sticks, these noodles vary in size from a narrow vermicelli style to a ribbon noodle about 5 mm wide. Made from rice flour, these noodles are served with spicy sauces and used in soups and stir-fry dishes. The noodles should be soaked before using; the narrow noodles require about 10 minutes soaking, while the wider ones will need about 30 minutes. These noodles are sometimes deep-fried, in which case there is no need to soak them. When fried, they puff up and become crisp.

Sesame paste: Made from sesame seeds, this is a rich, thick creamy-coloured paste, which is popular in the cooking of north and west China. If it is unavailable you can use peanut butter in its place.

Sesame seed oil: This strongly flavoured oil is used as a seasoning and is made from roasted sesame seeds. Usually added at the end of cooking. It is available from Asian food shops and keeps indefinitely.

Soy sauce: An essential ingredient for Chinese cooking. Soy sauce is made by fermenting soy beans with flour and water. It is then aged and distilled to make the resulting sauce. There are two types of soy sauce – light and sweet. The Chinese use light soy sauce for cooking. In Chinese food stores it is labelled Superior Soy. Sweet soy sauce is aged for longer than the light one, is slightly thicker and has a stronger flavour.

The Chinese prefer to use this sauce as a dipping sauce and for stews. In Chinese food stores it is labelled kecap manis (Sweet Sauce).

Straw mushrooms: These are available canned from Asian food stores. Before using, drain and rinse well.

Tofu: Also known as bean curd, tofu has played an important role in Chinese cooking for over a thousand years. It is made from yellow soy beans, which are soaked, ground and mixed with water, then briefly cooked before being solidified. It is rich in protein yet low in fat and cholesterol free.

Transparent noodles: Also called cellophane noodles, these noodles are added to Oriental soups and deep-fried as a garnish.

Water chestnuts: White, crunchy and about the size of a walnut, water chestnuts are a sweet root vegetable. Canned water chestnuts are available from Chinese food stores and some supermarkets. In China, fresh water chestnuts are boiled in their skins, then peeled and simmered with rock sugar and eaten as a snack. They are also popular in cooked dishes. When using canned water chestnuts, rinse them well first.

Wonton wrappers: These paper-thin pastry wrappers are available from Chinese food stores and some supermarkets.

Hot and sour soup

INGREDIENTS

4 cups water
2 tablespoons pickled chilli paste
2 tablespoons soy sauce
2 tablespoons rice wine vinegar
1½ teaspoons sugar
salt
½ teaspoon white pepper
2 tablespoons capsicum, deseeded
   and cut into 1 cm squares
2 tablespoons spring onions, cut into
   1 cm pieces
2 tablespoons carrots, chopped
¼ cup cabbage, chopped
1½ tablespoons cornflour
½ cup water
2 tablespoons tomato sauce
4 tablespoons lemon juice
serves 4

PREPARATION TIME
8 minutes

COOKING TIME
8 minutes

1 In a saucepan, mix water, chilli paste, soy sauce, vinegar, sugar, salt and pepper. Bring to the boil.

2 Add all the chopped vegetables. Cook for a minute on a medium heat. Dissolve cornflour in ½ cup water and add to the soup, stirring constantly until liquid thickens slightly. Cook for one more minute.

3 Stir through tomato sauce and serve soup immediately, topped with 1 tablespoon of lemon juice per bowl.

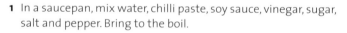

NUTRITIONAL VALUE PER SERVE	FAT 0.5 G	CARBOHYDRATE 9 G	PROTEIN 1.5 G

Indonesian coconut soup

INGREDIENTS

2 tablespoons olive oil
2 shallots, finely diced
4 garlic cloves, finely chopped
1 tablespoon ginger, finely diced
½ small red chilli, finely diced
1 stalk celery
1 medium carrot
2 cups pak choy, shredded
1.2 L chicken stock
200 ml coconut milk
200 ml coconut cream
1 tablespoon fish sauce
2 teaspoons lemongrass, finely sliced
½ teaspoon turmeric
100 g mungbean sprouts
100 g snowpeas, destringed
2 lemons, juiced
1 teaspoon salt
50 g fried shallots, to garnish
serves 4–6

1 Heat olive oil in a frying pan and fry shallots, garlic, ginger and chilli until golden: approximately 4 minutes.

2 Slice celery and carrot lengthways into thin strips. Add celery, carrot and pak choy to frying pan and cook for another 5 minutes.

3 Transfer vegetables to a medium saucepan. Add chicken stock, coconut milk, coconut cream, fish sauce, lemongrass and turmeric to pan.

4 Increase heat and bring to a simmer. Add mungbeans and snowpeas, stir and remove from heat.

5 Add lemon juice and salt to taste and serve and garnish with shallots.

PREPARATION TIME
15 minutes

COOKING TIME
20 minutes

NUTRITIONAL VALUE PER SERVE	FAT 24.5 G	CARBOHYDRATE 9 G	PROTEIN 5 G

Laksa

INGREDIENTS

paste

2 teaspoons shrimp paste
2 red onions, chopped
4 cloves garlic
zest of 1 lime
$\frac{1}{2}$ stalk lemongrass, sliced
1 tablespoon galangal, peeled and
  grated
6 birds-eye chillies, chopped
25 g candlenuts
1 teaspoon coriander seeds, toasted
2 coriander roots, chopped
1 teaspoon turmeric
1 tablespoon fresh coriander,
  chopped
$\frac{1}{2}$ cup oil

soup

2 cups chicken stock
2 cups coconut milk
4 puffed tofu, cut into quarters
350 g chicken breast, sliced thinly
12 prawns, shelled and deveined
125 g vermicelli rice noodles
250 g hokkien noodles
200 g snow peas, destringed
200 g green beans, topped and tailed
bean shoots, to garnish
fried shallots, to garnish
serves 4

1 To make the paste, dry roast the shrimp paste in
   a frying pan over a medium heat for 2 minutes.
   Put the shrimp paste in a food processor and add
   all the remaining paste ingredients to the food
   processor except the oil.

2 Blend ingredients to a smooth paste, adding the
   oil slowly.

3 To make the soup, heat a heavy-based saucepan,
   add 4 tablespoons of the paste, and fry for 3
   minutes. Add the stock and coconut milk to the
   saucepan and stir to combine. Bring to the boil
   and simmer for 10 minutes.

4 Add the tofu, chicken, prawns and noodles to
   the simmering soup. Cook for 5 minutes. Add
   the vegetables and cook for another 3 minutes.
   Remove from the heat. Divide the soup evenly
   between bowls and garnish with bean shoots
   and fried shallots.

PREPARATION TIME
45 minutes

COOKING TIME
20 minutes

NUTRITIONAL VALUE PER SERVE	FAT 50 G	CARBOHYDRATE 45 G	PROTEIN 40 G

Thai spice prawn soup

INGREDIENTS

1 tablespoon vegetable oil
550 g medium raw prawns, shelled
    and deveined, shells reserved
2 small red chillies, deseeded and cut
    into long thin strips
1 tablespoon paprika
¼ teaspoon ground red pepper
1.5 L chicken stock
2 cm strip lemon zest
2 cm strip lime zest
1 can straw mushrooms, drained
juice of 1 lemon
juice of ½ lime
2 tablespoons light soy sauce
small bunch fresh coriander, to
    garnish
serves 4

PREPARATION TIME
10 minutes

COOKING TIME
25 minutes

1 Heat wok over medium-high heat for 2 minutes. Add oil to wok: it should start to smoke. Carefully add prawns and 1 red chilli and stir-fry for 1 minute.

2 Add paprika and ground red pepper. Stir-fry for 1 minute longer. Remove prawn mixture and set aside.

3 Add prawn shells to wok and stir-fry for 2 minutes until shells turn orange. Add chicken stock and lemon and lime zest and bring to a boil. Cover, reduce heat and simmer for 15 minutes. Strain the soup and return the liquid to the saucepan.

4 Add mushrooms and prawn mixture to the soup and bring to a simmer. Stir in the lemon and lime juice, soy sauce and remaining red chilli. Serve garnished with fresh coriander.

NUTRITIONAL VALUE PER SERVE	FAT 7.5 G	CARBOHYDRATE 4 G	PROTEIN 35 G

Avocado, mango and papaya salad

INGREDIENTS

2 ripe avocados
juice of ½ lime
2 papayas
55 g mixed salad leaves
fresh coriander, to garnish
dressing
1 ripe mango
1 tablespoon rice wine vinegar or
   1 teaspoon white wine vinegar
juice of 1 lime
½ teaspoon sesame oil
1 cm fresh ginger, finely chopped
½ teaspoon clear honey
serves 4

1 To make the dressing, peel the mango, slice the flesh off the stone, then chop roughly. Blend to a thin purée with the vinegar, lime juice, oil, ginger and honey in a food processor. Alternatively, press the mango flesh through a sieve, then mix with the other dressing ingredients.

2 To make the salad, halve and peel the avocados, discarding the stones, then finely slice lengthways. Toss slices in the lime juice to stop them turning brown.

3 Halve the papayas, then scoop out and discard the seeds. Peel and finely slice the flesh. Arrange with the avocado and salad leaves on serving plates. Pour over the dressing and garnish with the coriander.

PREPARATION TIME
20 minutes

| NUTRITIONAL VALUE PER SERVE | FAT 28 G | CARBOHYDRATE 11 G | PROTEIN 3 G |

Spicy thai salad

INGREDIENTS

200 g green beans, sliced thinly
3 cucumbers, cut in half, deseeded
  and thinly sliced lengthways
2 mangos, diced
6 tablespoons palm sugar
6 teaspoons tamarind paste
2 teaspoons fish sauce
4 teaspoons water
paste
4 cloves garlic, chopped
4 chillies, chopped
½ teaspoon salt
1 lime
2 tablespoons roasted peanuts
4 tablespoons dried shrimp
12 cherry tomatoes, cut into quarters
serves 4

1 To make the paste, place garlic, chillies and salt in a mortar and pestle and pound. Remove and place in a bowl. Peel and dice the lime. Put the peanuts, lime and dried shrimp in the mortar and pestle and crush together. Add the cherry tomatoes and lightly mash into other ingredients.

2 Combine mixture carefully with the garlic and chilli paste.

3 In a large bowl, place green beans, cucumbers and mangos. Add the paste and gently combine. Mix together palm sugar, tamarind paste, fish sauce and water in a bowl and pour over the salad.

PREPARATION TIME
30 minutes

COOKING TIME
10 minutes

NUTRITIONAL VALUE PER SERVE	FAT 3 G	CARBOHYDRATE 45 G	PROTEIN 5 G

Burmese salad

INGREDIENTS

4 cloves garlic, finely chopped
2 tablespoons peanut oil
2 tablespoons green tea, brewed
juice of 1 lemon
1 tablespoon soy sauce
1½ tablespoons fish sauce
1 tablespoon ginger, grated
½ green chilli, deseeded and sliced
1 teaspoon palm sugar
2 tablespoons desiccated coconut
1 tablespoon sesame seeds
3 tablespoons peanuts, chopped
2 cups iceberg lettuce, shredded
1 cup tomato, diced
1 lemon, cut into wedges
serves 4

PREPARATION TIME
30 minutes

COOKING TIME
6 minutes

1   Preheat the oven to 180°C. Fry the garlic in peanut oil until
    light brown and crispy. Remove and drain off excess oil on
    kitchen towel.

2   To make the dressing, combine green tea, lemon juice, soy sauce,
    fish sauce, ginger, chilli and palm sugar with garlic in a bowl and
    set aside for 20 minutes.

3   Toast the coconut and sesame seeds separately in a frying pan
    until golden brown. Roast the peanuts in the oven until golden
    brown: approximately 3–4 minutes. Combine toasted nuts, seeds
    and coconut with shredded lettuce and tomato in a medium-
    sized bowl. Toss dressing through the salad. Serve with
    lemon wedges.

NUTRITIONAL VALUE PER SERVE	FAT 15 G	CARBOHYDRATE 4 G	PROTEIN 4 G

Chinese chilli and ginger-infused snapper

INGREDIENTS

2 whole snappers, scaled and cleaned
sea salt and ground black pepper
1 tablespoon sesame oil
20 g fresh ginger
1 long red chilli
2 spring onions
1 red capsicum
serves 2–4

PREPARATION TIME
7 minutes

COOKING TIME
15 minutes

1 Score fish on the diagonal. Rub sea salt and ground black pepper and oil into the fish, making sure it gets into the flesh.

2 Place the fish into the steamer.

3 Julienne the ginger and chilli and spread over the fish.

4 Steam for 12–15 minutes until fish is cooked. Garnish with julienned spring onions and red capsicum.

NUTRITIONAL VALUE PER SERVE	FAT 17 G	CARBOHYDRATE 1.5 G	PROTEIN 138 G

Red snapper with coconut sauce

INGREDIENTS

600 g red snapper
2 stems lemongrass, sliced
2 cm galangal, grated
6 cloves garlic, roughly chopped
1 shallot, roughly chopped
2 small red chillies, deseeded
2 kaffir lime leaves
2 tablespoons fresh dill
1 tablespoon sesame seeds
coconut sauce
1 can coconut milk
juice of 2 limes
2 tablespoons palm sugar
1 tablespoon fish sauce
serves 4

PREPARATION TIME
15 minutes

COOKING TIME
6 minutes

1 Combine all ingredients except snapper in a food processor and blend to a smooth paste.

2 Divide fish into four even portions. Remove any major bones. Score the fish and rub with paste, pressing into flesh. Set aside.

3 Prepare coconut sauce by combining coconut milk, lime juice, palm sugar and fish sauce in a small saucepan until warm and sugar has dissolved.

4 Heat a non-stick frying pan until very hot and cook fish, skin-side down, until golden brown. Turn and cook for 1 more minute. Serve with coconut sauce.

NUTRITIONAL VALUE PER SERVE	FAT 17.5 G	CARBOHYDRATE 11 G	PROTEIN 32 G

Korean stuffed prawns

INGREDIENTS

12 large prawns, shelled and deveined
1 teaspoon salt
120 g beef mince
2 teaspoons soy sauce
2 teaspoons spring onion, finely
  chopped
1 teaspoon garlic, finely chopped
½ teaspoon sugar
6 teaspoons sesame seed powder
3 teaspoons sesame oil
2 large banana leaves
1 cucumber
salt, extra
8 dried mushrooms, soaked, drained
  and finely sliced
1 teaspoon soy sauce
½ red capsicum, cut into thin strips
serves 4

1 Using a small sharp knife, make a long slit in the outside curve of each prawn and sprinkle with salt.

2 Mix the beef mince with soy sauce, spring onion, garlic, sugar, sesame seed powder and 1 teaspoon sesame oil.

3 Stuff the beef filling into the cuts made in the prawns. Wrap each prawn in a piece of banana leaf and secure with a skewer. Steam for approximately 15 minutes.

4 Wash cucumber skin, rub with salt and chop into 4 cm long pieces. Sprinkle with salt and mix with 1 teaspoon sesame oil.

5 Slice mushrooms finely and season with soy sauce and remaining sesame oil.

6 Serve steamed prawns on a bed of cucumber, mushroom and red capsicum strips.

PREPARATION TIME
20 minutes

COOKING TIME
15 minutes

NUTRITIONAL VALUE PER SERVE	FAT **5.6** G	CARBOHYDRATE **5.5** G	PROTEIN **19.5** G

Cashew and prawn fried rice

INGREDIENTS

350 g long-grain rice
425 ml water
salt
2 tablespoons peanut oil
1 clove garlic, finely chopped
1 cm fresh ginger, finely chopped
2 spring onions, sliced diagonally,
 white and green parts separated
50 g roasted salted cashews, chopped
75 g baby sweetcorn, cut into 1 cm
 lengths
200 g tiger prawns, cooked, peeled
2 tablespoons medium-dry sherry
3 tablespoons light soy sauce
2 teaspoons sesame oil
1 large egg, beaten
black pepper

serves 4

1 Rinse the rice, then place it in a large saucepan with water and salt. Bring to the boil, reduce the heat, then cover and simmer for 15 minutes. Drain, spread on a plate and leave to cool for 30 minutes, occasionally fluffing up with a fork.

2 Heat a wok or large frying pan and add the oil. Add the garlic, ginger and white parts of the spring onions and stir-fry for 1–2 minutes. Mix in the rice and stir-fry for 2 minutes.

3 Add the cashews and sweetcorn and stir-fry for 2 minutes. Add the prawns and sherry and stir-fry for 1 minute. Pour over the soy sauce and sesame oil and cook for a further 2 minutes.

4 Add the egg and stir-fry for 2–3 minutes. Season with black pepper and sprinkle with the green parts of the spring onions to serve.

PREPARATION TIME
15 minutes

COOKING TIME
25 minutes

NUTRITIONAL VALUE PER SERVE	FAT 18 G	CARBOHYDRATE 77 G	PROTEIN 21.5 G

Mussels with chilli and black bean

INGREDIENTS

3 teaspoons sugar
3 tablespoons soy sauce
4 tablespoons rice wine
1/2 cup water
2 red chillies
2 tablespoons oil
2 tablespoons fresh ginger, finely
  chopped
2 cloves garlic, finely chopped
4 spring onions, cut into 2 cm pieces
2 tablespoons fermented black
  beans, rinsed and crushed
1 kg black mussels, cleaned and
  debearded

serves 4

1 Combine sugar, soy sauce, rice wine and water in a bowl.

2 Cut the chillies in half lengthways. Heat the oil in a wok on a high heat. Add ginger, garlic, chillies, spring onions and black beans to the wok and fry for about 1 minute. Add the mussels to the wok, add the soy mix and toss the mussels to coat.

3 Cover and steam for approximately 4 minutes until the mussels open. Discard any mussels that do not open easily. Serve immediately.

PREPARATION TIME
5 minutes

COOKING TIME
25 minutes

| NUTRITIONAL VALUE PER SERVE | FAT 13.5 G | CARBOHYDRATE 18 G | PROTEIN 30.5 G |

Baby octopus salad

INGREDIENTS

2 teaspoons coriander seeds, toasted
2 cloves garlic, finely chopped
2 tablespoons lemon juice
4 tablespoons sweet chilli sauce
12 baby octopus
1 continental cucumber
1 bunch watercress, picked and
  washed
½ large red capsicum, thinly sliced
1 cup pickled ginger
1 tablespoon black sesame seeds
1 cup coriander leaves, picked and
  washed
1 cup bean shoots
1 cup canola oil
12 cloves garlic, thinly sliced

serves 4

1 To make marinade, grind coriander seeds in a mortar and pestle. Combine coriander seeds, garlic, lemon juice and sweet chilli sauce in a bowl. Marinate prepared baby octopus in refrigerator for 2 hours.

2 Using a vegetable peeler, peel thin lengthways strips of cucumber.

3 To make salad, combine watercress, cucumber, capsicum, pickled ginger, sesame seeds, coriander leaves and bean shoots in a large bowl. Set aside.

4 Heat oil in a frying pan and fry garlic until golden brown and crispy. Remove and drain on kitchen towel.

5 Strain the marinade from the octopus into a small saucepan and bring to a simmer. Set aside to cool. Heat a wok and stir-fry octopus until cooked: approximately 3–4 minutes.

6 Combine salad with octopus and toss through marinade. Serve garnished with crispy garlic.

PREPARATION TIME
15 minutes, plus
2 hours refrigeration

COOKING TIME
5 minutes

NUTRITIONAL VALUE PER SERVE · FAT 59.5 G · CARBOHYDRATE 6 G · PROTEIN 20 G

Japanese sake duck

INGREDIENTS

4 duck breasts
2 teaspoons salt
1 cup water
1 cup sake
1 cup plum juice
2 star anise
small bunch Asian greens
serves 4

PREPARATION TIME
2 hours refrigeration

COOKING TIME
12 minutes

1 Place duck breasts with the skin-side down on a tray, sprinkle with 1 teaspoon of salt and refrigerate for 2 hours.

2 Place duck in a steamer with water. Pour sake and plum juice over the duck, then add star anise to steaming liquid, close the lid tightly and steam for 7 minutes. Heat a small frying pan to moderately hot.

3 Remove duck from the steamer and set aside. Place Asian greens into steamer, cover again and steam for 3 minutes. Sear the duck skin in the frying pan for 2 minutes. Slice each breast into 4–5 pieces.

4 Remove the greens from the steamer and use as a bed for the slices of duck. Serve immediately.

NUTRITIONAL VALUE PER SERVE	FAT 39.5 G	CARBOHYDRATE 3 G	PROTEIN 30 G

Duck with crispy noodle pancakes

INGREDIENTS

¼ cup hoisin sauce
¼ cup light soy sauce
3 tablespoons sesame oil
6 cloves garlic, finely sliced
4 duck breasts
400 g packet rice stick noodles
1 cup shitake mushrooms, finely
  sliced
1 cup spring onions, finely sliced
2 cups canola oil
½ cup soy sauce, for dipping
coriander leaves, to garnish
serves 4

PREPARATION TIME
2 minutes, plus
2 hours marinating

COOKING TIME
25 minutes

1 Preheat the oven to 180°C. Combine hoisin sauce, soy sauce, 1
   tablespoon sesame oil and garlic in a bowl. Marinate duck breasts in
   the sauce for 1–2 hours.

2 Cook rice noodles as per packet instructions. Add mushrooms,
   spring onions and 1 tablespoon of sesame oil to noodles and
   set aside.

3 Heat remaining 1 tablespoon of sesame oil in a frying pan and
   seal duck breast, skin-side down first. Finish off cooking in oven for
   15 minutes. Remove duck from oven and rest for 5 minutes.

4 Heat the canola oil in frying pan. Cook rice noodle pancakes by
   placing 2 tablespoons of mixture into hot oil. Cook until golden,
   using a fork to help form the pancakes.

5 Slice the duck breast and serve with crispy noodle pancakes and soy
   sauce for dipping. Garnish with fresh coriander leaves.

NUTRITIONAL VALUE PER SERVE	FAT 171.8 G	CARBOHYDRATE 39 G	PROTEIN 36.5 G

Chilli duck with taro

INGREDIENTS

4 duck breasts
salt and pepper
2 small red chillies, finely chopped
2 large taros
2 tablespoons garlic, finely chopped
4 tablespoons honey
1 cup Chinese sherry
2 teaspoons sesame oil
4 tablespoons sugar
2 teaspoons sesame seeds, roasted,
  to garnish
serves 4

PREPARATION TIME
2 minutes, plus
1 hour refrigeration

COOKING TIME
15 minutes

1 Coat duck breasts with salt, pepper and chillies. Refrigerate for 1 hour.
   Preheat oven to 220°C and bring a medium-sized pot of water to the boil.
   Brush the chillies off the duck (keep chillies for sauce). In a frying pan sear
   the breasts skin-side down until the skin is an even medium-brown colour.
   Pour off, strain and reserve the excess fat. Place the breasts in the oven. Do
   not turn them. Cook 10–12 minutes, until medium rare.

2 Meanwhile, blanch the taros in the pot of boiling water for 1 minute, strain
   and pat dry with a tea towel. Coat taros with the reserved duck fat. Heat a
   small frying pan with garlic and honey, add the taros and cook for 3 minutes,
   then add to the oven with the duck.

3 Add the sherry, chillies, sesame oil and sugar to the frying pan and simmer.
   Reduce the liquid by half.

4 Remove duck and taros from the oven and leave to rest for 3 minutes. Slice
   the duck, serve it on top of the taros, spoon over the chilli–sherry sauce
   reduction and sprinkle with sesame seeds.

NUTRITIONAL VALUE PER SERVE	FAT 43.5 G	CARBOHYDRATE 62 G	PROTEIN 34 G

Chicken dumplings in chilli broth

INGREDIENTS

dumplings
300 g chicken breasts, diced
1 egg white
50 ml cream
2 shallots, finely diced
1 clove garlic
2 small red chillies
1 tablespoon sesame oil
1 tablespoon coriander, chopped
1 teaspoon fish sauce
1 teaspoon salt
1 teaspoon white pepper
chilli broth
1.5 L chicken stock
3 small red chillies, deseeded and
   cut lengthways
1 stem lemongrass, thinly sliced
20 g ginger, thinly sliced
coriander leaves, to garnish
serves 4–6

PREPARATION TIME
30 minutes

COOKING TIME
20 minutes

1 In a food processor, combine all the dumpling ingredients and process until the mix is smooth and well blended together.

2 Weigh out the dumpling mix into 15 g portions and roll into balls.

3 To make the chilli broth, place the ingredients into a saucepan. Bring to the boil and reduce to a simmer for 10 minutes. Place half the dumplings into the simmering broth and cook for 5 minutes.

4 Remove cooked dumplings with a slotted spoon and keep warm. Cook the remaining dumplings. To serve, place dumplings into bowls and pour over the broth. Garnish with coriander.

NUTRITIONAL VALUE PER SERVE	FAT 11.5 G	CARBOHYDRATE 1 G	PROTEIN 14.5 G

Chinese chilli chicken

INGREDIENTS

600 g boneless chicken
2 tablespoons soy sauce
2 tablespoons cornflour
1 tablespoon water
pinch of salt
1 egg
1½ cups oil
1 teaspoon garlic, finely chopped
6 green chillies, chopped with seeds
  left in
1½ cups chicken stock
1 teaspoon sugar
pinch of salt
½ teaspoon white pepper
3 spring onions, sliced into 1 cm
  pieces
serves 4

PREPARATION TIME
25 minutes

COOKING TIME
10 minutes

1 Cut the boneless chicken pieces into 2 cm cubes. Combine 1 tablespoon soy sauce,
   1 tablespoon cornflour, a pinch of salt and 1 egg in a bowl. Coat the chicken and marinate
   for 15 minutes.

2 Heat most of the oil, fry the chicken until just golden brown and set aside. Carefully
   remove most of the oil, leaving only about 1 tablespoon. Add the garlic and green chillies
   and fry for a few seconds.

3 Add 1½ cups of chicken stock. Bring to a simmer and add sugar, pepper, a pinch of salt, the
   rest of the soy sauce and half of the spring onions. Dissolve remaining cornflour in water
   and add to the sauce, stirring constantly. Reduce by half.

4 Add the chicken pieces and cook for a few minutes. Turn out onto a serving platter and
   garnish with the remaining spring onions.

NUTRITIONAL VALUE PER SERVE	FAT 98.5 G	CARBOHYDRATE 7 G	PROTEIN 44 G

Japanese eggplant with marinated chicken

INGREDIENTS

2 small- to medium-sized eggplants
2 cups rice wine vinegar
1 teaspoon salt
4 tablespoons light soy sauce
filling
200 g chicken mince
$^1/_2$ cup rice wine vinegar
1 red chilli, chopped
2 teaspoons sugar
$^1/_4$ teaspoon salt
4 tablespoons light soy sauce
white pepper
1 spring onion, finely sliced
2 teaspoons cornflour
serves 4

1 Cut the eggplants in half and scoop out the centres of each half with a sturdy spoon, leaving 1½ cm thickness of the flesh behind.

2 Dice the eggplant pieces that have been scooped out.

3 Combine eggplant pieces with the filling ingredients and allow to marinate for 15 minutes.

4 Put the following ingredients into the steamer and bring to the boil: 1½ cups rice vinegar, 1 teaspoon salt and 2 cups water.

5 Divide the filling among the eggplant halves and place them in the steamer. Pour an extra splash of rice wine vinegar and soy sauce over them, cover and steam for 20 minutes.

PREPARATION TIME
20 minutes

COOKING TIME
20 minutes

NUTRITIONAL VALUE PER SERVE	FAT 4.5 G	CARBOHYDRATE 15 G	PROTEIN 14 G

Red cooked chilli chicken

INGREDIENTS

1½ cups cold water
1½ cups dark soy sauce
¼ cup Chinese wine
2 cloves garlic, sliced
2 large red chillies
2 star anise
1½ tablespoons palm sugar
50 g ginger
1 small roasting chicken
2 teaspoons sesame oil
serves 4

1 Place all the ingredients except the chicken and sesame oil in a bowl. Stir to combine. Place the chicken in the marinade and refrigerate for 2–3 hours or overnight.

2 Remove the chicken from the marinade. Place chicken, breast down, in a large saucepan over a low heat.

3 Pour the marinade over the chicken and bring to the boil slowly. Reduce the heat, cover and simmer for 15 minutes. Turn the chicken over and simmer for a further 20 minutes.

4 Remove the pan from the heat, cover and let it cool. Once cooled, remove the chicken from the liquid and cut it into pieces. Brush the pieces with the sesame oil.

5 Reserve the cooking liquid as a dipping sauce.

PREPARATION TIME
5 minutes, plus 2–3 hours refrigeration

COOKING TIME
40 minutes

NUTRITIONAL VALUE PER SERVE	FAT 37.5 G	CARBOHYDRATE 9 G	PROTEIN 49 G

Chicken and snowpea noodles

INGREDIENTS

250 g dried egg thread noodles
2 tablespoons peanut oil
1 red or yellow capsicum, deseeded
  and chopped
1 cm fresh ginger, finely chopped
1 clove garlic, finely chopped
2 spring onions, cut into 2.5 cm
  lengths, white and green parts
  separated
2 skinless chicken breast fillets, cut
  into strips
170 g snowpeas
2 tablespoons dark soy sauce
1 tablespoon oyster sauce
serves 4

PREPARATION TIME
20 minutes

COOKING TIME
12 minutes

1 Cook the noodles according to the packet instructions. Drain
   and rinse.

2 Heat a wok, then add the oil. Stir-fry the capsicum, ginger, garlic
   and white parts of the spring onions for 1 minute. Add the chicken
   and stir-fry for 5 minutes.

3 Add the snowpeas to the wok and stir-fry for 1 minute. Add the
   noodles and green parts of the spring onions, mixing well, then
   stir in the soy and oyster sauces. Stir-fry for 5 minutes or until the
   chicken is cooked through.

NUTRITIONAL VALUE PER SERVE	FAT 19.5 G	CARBOHYDRATE 37 G	PROTEIN 45 G

Quail with spice glaze

INGREDIENTS

4 quails
80 g butter, melted
3 tablespoons soy sauce
3 tablespoons honey
4 small cinnamon sticks
4 star anise
5 cardamon pods, bruised
5 cloves garlic, finely sliced
serves 4

PREPARATION TIME
10 minutes

COOKING TIME
15 minutes

1 Preheat the oven to 200°C. Open quails out by placing them breast down on a chopping board and removing the backbone and ribcage. Set aside.

2 Combine the butter, soy sauce, honey, cinnamon sticks, star anise, cardamom pods and garlic in a bowl.

3 Place quails on a roasting tray with breasts facing up. Coat with the spice mix glaze. Bake for 15 minutes, turning once.

NUTRITIONAL VALUE PER SERVE   FAT **24** G   CARBOHYDRATE **19** G   PROTEIN **22.5** G

Garlic beef with ginger

INGREDIENTS

800 g beef fillet
8 cloves garlic, finely chopped
½ cup kecap manis
1 tablespoon ginger, grated
1 Thai red chilli, sliced
1 tablespoon sesame oil
1 tablespoon palm sugar
juice of 2 limes
1 bunch bok choy
1 bunch Chinese broccoli
400 g packet rice noodle sticks
1 teaspoon cornflour
1 teaspoon water
serves 4

PREPARATION TIME
10 minutes, plus
overnight refrigeration

COOKING TIME
10 minutes

1 Clean beef fillet of sinew and excess fat. To make marinade, combine
    garlic, kecap manis, ginger, chilli, sesame oil, palm sugar and lime juice
    in a bowl. Marinate beef fillet overnight in refrigerator.

2 Prepare vegetables by discarding outer leaves and washing, then set
    aside. Heat a large frying pan until almost smoking and sear beef fillet
    until brown on all sides. Reserve marinade.

3 Cook rice noodles as per packet instructions. Stir-fry the Asian greens in
    a hot wok and set aside. Add reserved marinade to the wok and bring
    to a simmer.

4 Mix cornflour with water, add to the wok and reduce heat. Thinly slice
    the beef. Serve the beef on top of rice noodles, bok choy and Chinese
    broccoli and drizzle with sauce.

NUTRITIONAL VALUE PER SERVE	FAT 15 G	CARBOHYDRATE 27 G	PROTEIN 45.5 G

Braised beef in soy

INGREDIENTS

6 tablespoons coriander seeds
4 tablespoons water
1½ cups shallots, finely diced
12 cloves garlic, chopped
2 tablespoons oil
2 sticks cinnamon
6 tablespoons soybean paste, mashed
4 tablespoons sugar
1 teaspoon ground cloves
8 small beef shins
3 tablespoons dark soy sauce
2 L water
150 g canned bamboo shoots, drained
salt and pepper
1 large red chilli, julienned, to garnish
watercress, to garnish
serves 4

1 Grind the coriander seeds in a mortar and pestle and mix with 4 tablespoons of water. Purée the shallots and garlic in a food processor. Heat oil in a large saucepan and fry the shallot purée with cinnamon sticks until golden. Add coriander mixture, mashed soybean paste, sugar and cloves and cook for two minutes.

2 Increase the heat and add the beef, cooking until browned. Add soy sauce and 2 litres of water and bring to the boil, stirring occasionally. Reduce heat and simmer, partly covered, until meat is tender: approximately 2½ hours. Remove beef from liquid and set aside.

3 Reduce the liquid to sauce consistency. Return beef to sauce and add bamboo shoots. Discard the cinnamon sticks and season with salt and pepper. Garnish with red chilli and watercress.

PREPARATION TIME
10 minutes

COOKING TIME
3 hours

NUTRITIONAL VALUE PER SERVE	FAT 13 G	CARBOHYDRATE 23 G	PROTEIN 72 G

Teriyaki pork spare ribs

INGREDIENTS

12 pork ribs, cut into 5 cm pieces
2 teaspoons salt
2 teaspoons freshly ground black pepper
2 tablespoons canola oil
5 large onions, roughly chopped
3 cups carrot, roughly chopped
3 cups celery, roughly chopped
2 medium fennel bulbs, chopped
4 stems lemongrass, finely chopped
5 tablespoons garlic, finely chopped
1 tablespoon ginger, grated
1 cup teriyaki sauce
2 cups Chinese sherry
1½ cups dark soy sauce
6 sprigs thyme
3 dried bay leaves
2 cups water
serves 4

1 Sprinkle ribs with salt and pepper. Heat oil in a large frying pan and sear ribs until brown: approximately 10–15 minutes. Remove ribs and set aside.

2 Add onions, carrots, celery, fennel, lemongrass, garlic and ginger to frying pan and fry until soft. Add teriyaki sauce, sherry, soy sauce, thyme and bay leaves.

3 Transfer vegetables into a large saucepan. Return ribs to the vegetable mixture and add the water. Bring to the boil and then reduce heat to a simmer.

4 Cover and cook for 3 hours or until ribs are very tender. Remove ribs and set aside. Reduce liquid by a third or to a glaze consistency and pour over the ribs before serving.

PREPARATION TIME
20 minutes

COOKING TIME
3 hours 30 minutes

NUTRITIONAL VALUE PER SERVE	FAT 23.5 G	CARBOHYDRATE 46 G	PROTEIN 44.5 G

Cantonese honey-glazed pork

INGREDIENTS

500 g rindless boneless pork loin, cut
  into 5 cm pieces
marinade
2 cloves garlic
1 teaspoon salt
2 tablespoons light soy sauce
3 tablespoons sugar
1 tablespoon rice wine or
  medium-dry sherry
1 teaspoon five spice powder
  (optional)
1 teaspoon hoisin sauce
1 tablespoon clear honey
serves 4

PREPARATION TIME
10 minutes, plus
4 hours refrigeration

COOKING TIME
1 hour

1 To make the marinade, crush the garlic with the salt, then mix
   with the rest of the marinade ingredients in a non-metallic bowl.
   Score each piece of pork a few times with a sharp knife, add to the
   marinade and turn to coat. Cover and refrigerate for 4 hours or
   overnight, turning occasionally.

2 Preheat the oven to 200°C. Half-fill a deep roasting tin with
   boiling water and place the pork on a rack over the top, ensuring
   that the meat does not touch the water. Brush the pork with half
   the marinade and roast for 30 minutes.

3 Reduce the heat to 180°C. Turn the pork over and brush with the
   remaining marinade. Roast for another 30 minutes until the pork
   is cooked through and tender. Slice into 1 cm thick pieces to serve.

NUTRITIONAL VALUE PER SERVE   FAT 7.5 G   CARBOHYDRATE 20 G   PROTEIN 36.5 G

Chinese chilli pork

INGREDIENTS

360 g pork mince
1 tablespoon dark soy sauce
2 tablespoons Chinese sherry
1 tablespoon hoisin sauce
1/3 cup chicken stock
2 tablespoons Chinese sherry
1 tablespoon hoisin sauce
1 tablespoon oyster sauce
1 tablespoon bean sauce
1/2 tablespoon sesame oil
1/2 tablespoon white vinegar
1 tablespoon Chinese chilli sauce
2 tablespoons cornflour
2 tablespoons peanut oil
2 tablespoons ginger, finely chopped
3 cloves garlic, finely chopped
1 green capsicum, deseeded and cut
　　into 2 cm squares
1 red capsicum, deseeded and cut
　　into 2 cm squares
1 yellow capsicum, deseeded and cut
　　into 2 cm squares
1 onion, coarsely chopped
spring onions, chopped, to garnish
3 red chillies, deseeded and chopped,
　　to garnish
serves 4

1　Combine pork, soy sauce, sherry and hoisin sauce in a bowl. Set aside to marinate.

2　In a small bowl, combine the chicken stock, sherry, hoisin sauce, oyster sauce, bean sauce, sesame oil, vinegar and chilli sauce. Set aside this sauce. Stir cornflour into an equal amount of cold water, then set aside.

3　Heat wok until very hot, add 1 tablespoon peanut oil and wait until it begins to smoke. Add pork and stir-fry, for about 3 minutes. Transfer to a bowl.

4　Return wok to very high heat and add remaining peanut oil. Add ginger and garlic and cook for a few seconds. Add vegetables and stir-fry until onion becomes transparent, approximately 2 minutes. Return pork to wok and add the sauce. Bring sauce to a simmer, stir in a little cornflour mixture to thicken slightly. Serve topped with sliced spring onions and chillies.

PREPARATION TIME
12 minutes

COOKING TIME
10 minutes

NUTRITIONAL VALUE PER SERVE	FAT 20 G	CARBOHYDRATE 17 G	PROTEIN 21 G

Chinese pork buns

INGREDIENTS

1½ teaspoons dried yeast
2 tablespoons sugar
1 cup warm water
2½ cups plain flour
1 teaspoon salt
2 tablespoons peanut oil
2 shallots, finely diced
2 teaspoons garlic, crushed
250 g pork fillet, cut into cubes
2 tablespoons oyster sauce
2 tablespoons soy sauce
2 tablespoons char sui sauce
2 tablespoons Chinese rice wine
1½ teaspoons baking powder
makes 10–12 buns

PREPARATION TIME
3½ hours

COOKING TIME
10 minutes

1 Place the yeast into a bowl with the sugar and warm water. Leave in warm draught-free place until frothy (about 10 minutes).

2 Sift the flour and salt into a large bowl. Make a well in the middle and add 1 tablespoon of the peanut oil and the yeast mixture to form a dough.

3 Knead the dough for approximately 10 minutes, until smooth and elastic. Place the dough in an oiled bowl, cover and leave to rise for 2–3 hours until doubled in size.

4 In a pan or wok, heat the remaining oil, then add shallots, garlic and pork. Cook for a few minutes, then add sauces and rice wine. Remove from heat when pork is cooked.

5 Place dough onto a floured surface, press out to form a circle, sprinkle with baking powder, fold up and knead for 5 minutes.

6 Divide the dough up into 10–12 even pieces; roll each piece out to a 10 cm circle.

7 Place a tablespoon of filling into the centre of each circle, gather up the edges around the filling, bring together and twist securely.

8 Place the buns onto squares of greaseproof paper and into steamer. Allow to rise for another half an hour, then steam over rapidly boiling water for approximately 10 minutes.

NUTRITIONAL VALUE PER SERVE	FAT 4.5 G	CARBOHYDRATE 27 G	PROTEIN 9 G

Rice powder lamb

INGREDIENTS

800 g boneless lamb pieces
3 teaspoons soy sauce
1 teaspoon salt
$\frac{1}{2}$ teaspoon sugar
12 slices ginger
4 garlic cloves, crushed
2 spring onions, roughly chopped and
  lightly crushed
2 small dried chillies, ground
$\frac{1}{2}$ cup uncooked long-grain rice
1 star anise
fresh banana leaves

serves 4

1 Pound the lamb with a mallet, to create an even thickness and cut into bite-sized pieces.

2 Mix the meat with the soy sauce, salt, sugar, half of the ginger, garlic, spring onions and chillies and set aside to marinade for 30 minutes.

3 Prepare the rice powder by putting the rice and the star anise into a dry frying pan on a medium-high heat. Dry-fry until brown, stirring constantly.

4 Cool slightly and blend rice in a blender to the consistency of fine sand, being careful not to overblend.

5 Liberally coat the meat in the rice powder, then place a banana leaf on the bottom of a steamer and cover with lamb pieces. Add another banana leaf and cover with more lamb pieces. Add the remaining ginger pieces to the steamer water and steam for 25 minutes.

PREPARATION TIME
50 minutes

COOKING TIME
25 minutes

NUTRITIONAL VALUE PER SERVE	FAT **14** G	CARBOHYDRATE **22** G	PROTEIN **44** G

Glossary

Al dente: Italian term to describe pasta and rice that are cooked until tender but still firm to the bite.

Asafoetida: a herbaceous perennial plant native to Iran. The dried sap is used as a spice. It resembles onion and garlic in flavour.

Bake blind: to bake pastry cases without their fillings. Line the raw pastry case with greaseproof paper and fill with raw rice or dried beans to prevent collapsed sides and puffed base. Remove paper and fill 5 minutes before completion of cooking time.

Baste: to spoon hot cooking liquid over food at intervals during cooking to moisten and flavour it.

Beat: to make a mixture smooth with rapid and regular motions using a spatula, wire whisk or electric mixer; to make a mixture light and smooth by enclosing air.

Beurre manié: equal quantities of butter and flour mixed together to a smooth paste and stirred bit by bit into a soup, stew or sauce while on the heat to thicken. Stop adding when desired thickness results.

Bind: to add egg or a thick sauce to hold ingredients together when cooked.

Blanch: to plunge some foods into boiling water for less than a minute and immediately plunge into iced water. This is to brighten the colour of some vegetables; to remove skin from tomatoes and nuts.

Blend: to mix 2 or more ingredients thoroughly together; do not confuse with blending in an electric blender.

Boil: to cook in a liquid brought to boiling point and kept there.

Boiling point: when bubbles rise continually and break over the entire surface of the liquid, reaching a temperature of 100°C (212°F). In some cases food is held at this high temperature for a few seconds then heat is turned to low for slower cooking. See simmer.

Bouquet garni: a bundle of several herbs tied together with string for easy removal, placed into pots of stock, soups and stews for flavour. A few sprigs of fresh thyme, parsley and bay leaf are used. Can be purchased in sachet form for convenience.

Caramelise: to heat sugar in a heavy-based pan until it liquefies and develops a caramel colour. Vegetables such as blanched carrots and sautéed onions may be sprinkled with sugar and caramelised.

Chill: to place in the refrigerator or stir over ice until cold.

Clarify: to make a liquid clear by removing sediments and impurities. To melt fat and remove any sediment.

Coat: to dust or roll food items in flour to cover the surface before the food is cooked. Also, to coat in flour, egg and breadcrumbs.

Cool: to stand at room temperature until some or all heat is removed, e.g. cool a little, cool completely.

Cream: to make creamy and fluffy by working the mixture with the back of a wooden spoon, usually refers to creaming butter and sugar or margarine. May also be creamed with an electric mixer.

Croutons: small cubes of bread, toasted or fried, used as an addition to salads or as a garnish to soups and stews.

Crudite: raw vegetable sticks served with a dipping sauce.

Crumb: to coat foods in flour, egg and breadcrumbs to form a protective coating for foods which are fried. Also adds flavour, texture and enhances appearance.

Cube: to cut into small pieces with six even sides, e.g. cubes of meat.

Cut in: to combine fat and flour using 2 knives scissor fashion or with a pastry blender, to make pastry.

Deglaze: to dissolve dried out cooking juices left on the base and sides of a roasting dish or frying pan. Add a little water, wine or stock, scrape and stir over heat until dissolved. Resulting liquid is used to make a flavoursome gravy or added to a sauce or casserole.

Degrease: to skim fat from the surface of cooking liquids, e.g. stocks, soups, casseroles.

Dice: to cut into small cubes.

Dredge: to heavily coat with icing sugar, sugar, flour or cornflour.

Dressing: a mixture added to completed dishes to add moisture and flavour, e.g. salads, cooked vegetables.

Drizzle: to pour in a fine thread-like stream moving over a surface.

Egg wash: beaten egg with milk or water used to brush over pastry, bread dough or biscuits to give a sheen and golden brown colour.

Essence: a strong flavouring liquid, usually made by distillation. Only a few drops are needed to flavour.

Fillet: a piece of prime meat, fish or poultry which is boneless or has all bones removed.

Flake: to separate cooked fish into flakes, removing any bones and skin, using 2 forks.

Flame: to ignite warmed alcohol over food or to pour into a pan with food, ignite then serve.

Flute: to make decorative indentations around the pastry rim before baking.

Fold in: combining of a light, whisked or creamed mixture with other ingredients. Add a portion of the other ingredients at a time and mix using a gentle circular motion, over and under the mixture so that air will not be lost. Use a silver spoon or spatula.

Glaze: to brush or coat food with a liquid that will give the finished product a glossy appearance, and on baked products, a golden brown colour.

Grease: to rub the surface of a metal or heatproof dish with oil or fat, to prevent the food from sticking.

Herbed butter: softened butter mixed with finely chopped fresh herbs and re-chilled. Used to serve on grilled meats and fish.

Hors d'oeuvre: small savoury foods served as an appetiser, popularly known today as 'finger food'.

Infuse: to steep foods in a liquid until the liquid absorbs their flavour.

Joint: to cut poultry and game into serving pieces by dividing at the joint.

Julienne: to cut some food, e.g. vegetables and processed meats, into fine strips the length of matchsticks. Used for inclusion in salads or as a garnish to cooked dishes.

Knead: to work a yeast dough in a pressing, stretching and folding motion with the heel of the hand until smooth and elastic to develop the gluten strands. Non-yeast doughs should be lightly and quickly handled as gluten development is not desired.

Line: to cover the inside of a baking tin with paper for the easy removal of the cooked product from the baking tin.

Macerate: to stand fruit in a syrup, liqueur or spirit to give added flavour.

Marinade: a flavoured liquid, into which food is placed for some time to give it flavour and to tenderise. Marinades include an acid ingredient such as vinegar or wine, oil and seasonings.

Mask: to evenly cover cooked food portions with a sauce, mayonnaise or savoury jelly.

Pan-fry: to fry foods in a small amount of fat or oil, sufficient to coat the base of the pan.

Parboil: to boil until partially cooked. The food is then finished by some other method.

Pare: to peel the skin from vegetables and fruit. Peel is the popular term but pare is the name given to the knife used; paring knife.

Pit: to remove stones or seeds from olives, cherries, dates.

Pith: the white lining between the rind and flesh of oranges, grapefruit and lemons.

Pitted: the olives, cherries, dates etc. with the stone removed, e.g. purchase pitted dates.

Poach: to simmer gently in enough hot liquid to almost cover the food so shape will be retained.

Pound: to flatten meats with a meat mallet; to reduce to a paste or small particles with a mortar and pestle.

Simmer: to cook in liquid just below boiling point at about 96°C (205°F) with small bubbles rising gently to the surface.

Skim: to remove fat or froth from the surface of simmering food.

Stock: the liquid produced when meat, poultry, fish or vegetables have been simmered in water to extract the flavour. Used as a base for soups, sauces, casseroles etc. Convenience stock products are available.

Sweat: to cook sliced onions or vegetables, in a small amount of butter in a covered pan over low heat, to soften them and release flavour without colouring.

Conversions

Measurements differ from country to country, so it's important to understand what the differences are. This Measurements Guide gives you simple 'at-a-glance' information for using the recipes in this book, wherever you may be.

Cooking is not an exact science – minor variations in measurements won't make a difference to your cooking.

EQUIPMENT

There is a difference in the size of measuring cups used internationally, but the difference is minimal (only 2–3 teaspoons). We use the Australian standard metric measurements in our recipes:

1 teaspoon ....5 ml	1 tablespoon....20 ml
1/2 cup......125 ml	1 cup.....250 ml
4 cups...1 litre	

Measuring cups come in sets of one cup (250 ml), 1/2 cup (125 ml), 1/3 cup (80 ml) and 1/4 cup (60 ml). Use these for measuring liquids and certain dry ingredients.

Measuring spoons come in a set of four and should be used for measuring dry and liquid ingredients.

When using cup or spoon measures always make them level (unless the recipe indicates otherwise).

DRY VERSUS WET INGREDIENTS

While this system of measures is consistent for liquids, it's more difficult to quantify dry ingredients. For instance, one level cup equals: 200 g of brown sugar; 210 g of caster sugar; and 110 g of icing sugar.

When measuring dry ingredients such as flour, don't push the flour down or shake it into the cup. It is best just to spoon the flour in until it reaches the desired amount. When measuring liquids use a clear vessel indicating metric levels.

Always use medium eggs (55–60 g) when eggs are required in a recipe.

OVEN

Your oven should always be at the right temperature before placing the food in it to be cooked. Note that if your oven doesn't have a fan you may need to cook food for a little longer.

MICROWAVE

It is difficult to give an exact cooking time for microwave cooking. It is best to watch what you are cooking closely to monitor its progress.

STANDING TIME

Many foods continue to cook when you take them out of the oven or microwave. If a recipe states that the food needs to 'stand' after cooking, be sure not to overcook the dish.

CAN SIZES

The can sizes available in your supermarket or grocery store may not be the same as specified in the recipe. Don't worry if there is a small variation in size – it's unlikely to make a difference to the end result.

dry		liquids	
metric (grams)	imperial (ounces)	metric (millilitres)	imperial (fluid ounces)
		30 ml	1 fl oz
30 g	1 oz	60 ml	2 fl oz
60 g	2 oz	90 ml	3 fl oz
90 g	3 oz	100 ml	3 1/2 fl oz
100 g	3 1/2 oz	125 ml	4 fl oz
125 g	4 oz	150 ml	5 fl oz
150 g	5 oz	190 ml	6 fl oz
185 g	6 oz	250 ml	8 fl oz
200 g	7 oz	300 ml	10 fl oz
250 g	8 oz	500 ml	16 fl oz
280 g	9 oz	600 ml	20 fl oz (1 pint)*
315 g	10 oz	1000 ml (1 litre)	32 fl oz
330 g	11 oz		
370 g	12 oz		
400 g	13 oz		
440 g	14 oz		
470 g	15 oz		
500 g	16 oz (1 lb)		
750 g	24 oz (1 1/2 lb)		
1000 g (1 kg)	32 oz (2 lb)		*Note: an American pint is 16 fl oz.

cooking temperatures	°C (celsius)	°F (fahrenheit)	gas mark
very slow	120	250	1/2
slow	150	300	2
moderately slow	160	315	2–3
moderate	180	350	4
moderate hot	190	375	5
	200	400	6
hot	220	425	7
very hot	230	450	8
	240	475	9
	250	500	10

Index